Stray Gods

poems by

Carolyn Supinka

Finishing Line Press
Georgetown, Kentucky

Stray Gods

Copyright © 2016 by Carolyn Supinka
ISBN 978-1-944899-65-3 First Edition
All rights reserved under International and Pan-American Copyright Conventions.
No part of this book may be reproduced in any manner whatsoever without written permission from the publisher, except in the case of brief quotations embodied in critical articles and reviews.

ACKNOWLEDGMENTS

Previously published poems:

The Maynard: Girl I, Girl II
Stirring: A Literary Collection: Body
Poet Lore: The Way Back, Vernacular Home * nominated for the Pushcart Prize 2016, Stare Hypothetical
Vayavya: Banana Leaf Scripture, Confession

Publisher: Leah Maines

Editor: Christen Kincaid

Cover Art: Kim and Jessica Magnan

Author Photo: Irene Gomez Emilsson

Cover Design: Elizabeth Maines

Printed in the USA on acid-free paper.
Order online: www.finishinglinepress.com
also available on amazon.com

Author inquiries and mail orders:
Finishing Line Press
P. O. Box 1626
Georgetown, Kentucky 40324
U. S. A.

Table of Contents

Dog On The Roof 1
Free Indian Philosophy, Three Times A Week 2
Bird Seller In A Monsoon.. 3
Natural Worship 4
Vernacular Home 5
Letters From A New House... 6
Stare Hypothetical 7
Fair Ever.. 8
Market Dissection 9
The Call.. 10
He Used To Be George 11
Catalogue... 12
Every Clean Beast... 13
Drongo Ode 14
Confession... 15
Banana Leaf Scripture 16
Body 17
We Were There At The Start And Saw How It Would Go ... 18
Making Breakfast After A Home Invasion........................... 19
Resource 21
High Definition...22
Girl I 23
Girl II..24
Girl III 25
The Way Back..26

Thank you to Dr. Murali Sivaramakrishnan, Tejaswi Murali, Dr. Usha Murali, to all of the English Department at Pondicherry University, to George at Jovial Travels, to John and B. and Rachel and Mani and Ju and Chandru and Soumya and Mr. and Mrs. Rao, to Manasa and Anu Suresh, to Jim Daniels and Yona Harvey, to Usha Iyer at the Pearl Academy, to Kim Magnan and Benoit Ralu.

Thank you to my family, to Jordan, to Katie and Clare and Morgan and Julie, to Max, to the Sri Aurobindo Library and Shiva at the Sri Aurobindo Society, to Dr. Renuka Gurung, to Jasneet and Rohini and Phoebe and Sara, to Neeraj Goswami and Vinita Tripathi and the Fulbright Program.

Dog On The Roof
For the strays of South India

The dogs here are warnings. Long-necked
Anubis stalks the streets, red eyed
stray god cast down from some cruel
Olympus, the latch locked,
the kitchen door slammed shut.
I bet the other gods are laughing
that you are on the streets, dog.
Gods without a home are free
to wander at will. The stray gods
slip through the streets, cast their slit
eyed gaze at passing cabs and rickshaws,
eat the refuse of the people, and watch.

Free Indian Philosophy Three Times A Week

He said, *when you are destroyed*
and it was like last spring

in Pittsburgh on a wet black road reaching
a thin arm down

from a hilltop to the river, also black
with white streaks curling silently.

The only sign of winter
is being strangled

below the surface, seasonal murder
and healthy transitions.

The professor is from the North
and he leaves four times every year
to take a train to visit his mother.
No one speaks Hindi with him here
in the South.

I try, but all I can say is *hello* and *how are you*
and *mother* and *my name is* and *how can I go*.

He said, *when you are destroyed*
and I could only think of the river,

and the rocks that I would throw
to break the smoky surface

and the shock I felt when the chaos
revealed itself, churning below.

Bird Seller In A Monsoon

A person about to cross a river.
Paper floats downstream, correspondence trash
wallows between my legs. Pulpy letter trail.
A candle flickers at the edge of vision
and seems to go out. If you are truly here,
tell me: is my face ashen?
What is the color of my skin? Downstream
has washed me out. This excuse for a memory.
I think of yesterday as a dirty river, the flow
eroding earth beneath my feet. It threatens
to soak my slippers.
It threatens to steep my feet,
to sink me. I think of yesterday
like the man selling parakeet fortunes
on the side of the road, training the exotic to speak
for pennies. Their tails are crooked, crushed
into the shape of a fan, a future spreading
in sticky fibers. Six to a cage.

Natural Worship

On the steps of the temple
the test begins. Nobody needs to tell you
that you don't belong. The sticky residue
of something else is evident in your footprints.
It covers the ring of rich sugar around your lips.
You are not some unfed pilgrim. You are not
some angel, starving for crumbs. You relish toast
and honey, and it might be the yeast that suffocates
worldly understanding. You are not a saint,
but you might be a plant.

When you approach the altar, the tilt of your head
takes on the aspect of a frozen tree's spine,
arching under a natural punishment: the desire
to receive a blessing. Found out!
A chase scene commences and we disperse
through the bamboo forest on stage left.
How exotic. The priest tries out three languages
and settles on his own. The second question
forms a nation: Which country?
And it's the easiest to answer.

Vernacular Home

In the belly of summer
we walk through red fields
and watch a village burn. *Scrub.*

They are famous
for this, one boy says, points
at the plain. A long hot snake
winds at the horizon;
it's easy to imagine the land
squeezing the life out of you.

As a child, I built houses
out of sticks and twine,
little wooden pyramids
testing the meaning of the word. *Shelter.*
The simplest terms of life. I pretended
I had been a hermit for years,
eating miraculous berries (blue,
deathless sustenance!), befriending
young deer. I pretended I'd died there,
and my nest became a grave,
and in the evening, I resurrected myself.

The boy: Can you believe –huts!
I believe huts. I believe in huts
and heat, the dark doorway,
the threshold between out and in.

Letters From A New House

Love, the floors here are cold and smooth. Fake marble the color
of a forgotten pond, misty with algae cloud. I used to think it was strange,
but now I cannot imagine the floor being anything else.
It makes sweeping easy. It makes slipping easy.
It makes the noises from the streets echo.
When the Muslim man rides by on his bicycle, selling mats,
his wheels creak through the kitchen, across the living room,
and into the hallway. If I close my eyes he is riding circles
around me, and I open my eyes to an empty room
and a light dusting of dry yellow straw.

Love, I thought the house next door was empty, but it's not. Last night
I heard coughing echoing from the black windows
and somebody walking through the gravel
on the lawn. To be sick and alone in a house,
to find yourself alone in your own yard at night. At night, the street
is an underwater chasm. I dream of floating out the front door
and drifting to the edge, looking down into the black hole.
I can keep my back straight, I can turn, point my chin at the ground,
I can pencil dive off of my stoop and into the night.

Love, I wish there was more light. I think I know your face best
when it is half lit, when we are in a dark room in a sleeping city
and the harsh white light comes in from the street and licks bold strokes
across the long line of your nose, the dark territory
where your eyebrows touch unhappiness.

Love, I don't think this is working.
At least three days have passed
and your presence has become less than a ghost.
Half of a ghost is a voice,
any less than that and you are a shade.
I see you moving next to me
in the shadow of the trees I'm climbing. You,
who are so firmly rooted to the earth
I can't imagine you climbing with me.
Yesterday, two little boys stole ripe
fruit from this tree and left the unripe for us.
I heard rustling and thought it was a bird,
but a boy leapt from the branches to run across the garden,
and he flew over the wall.

Stare Hypothetical

Along the canal a bus floats past.
Vehicular cannon volley.
      A man presses his face to the glass,
      submerged sight, that poignant periscope

of cupped hands and wide eyes.
To say that his gaze is violent
      is to presuppose. He could be a puppet,
      floppy head directed at my legs

which are sweating through a green skirt.
Arbitrary mechanics.
      Puppet swears at puppeteer.
      Audience laughs.

I want to shake that great magician,
rattle some curtains. To say a look
      is suggestive is to hypothesize.
      Had I a lab, I could dissect. Off with the head.

Off with the collared shirt, the dirty fingernails.
I hypothesize dirty fingernails, but the shirt is fact.
      Off with the daylight, I could squint better
      by the moon, could murmur the anatomy

perfectly, and if given a chance to press my face
to the glass, I could look back,
      rally a conclusion,
find answers in a stranger's body.

Fair Ever

Reaching across the pile
of rotting plantains, a brown
veined resumption of pre-birth,
she cups my face, her fingers
thick and dark, rough as ocean rocks.
"Good," pronounced, judging a fruit
ripe or rotten. Whatever reply
I stammer is forgotten. My face weighed
at a market place next to the rice
and skirts, and deemed worthy.
What mirror can I hold to this?
Such a statement of fact. I could dream
of a new life as a fruit, engineered
to bloom on command.

Market Dissection

The green curvatures,
dull suede skins edged
with a yellow siphoned straight
from the shining bangles of the woman
piling melons on the roadside, a pyramid
of little earths. No mercy. She wields a knife
straight as the thin line of her mouth,
slices with a snick and a pop, produces
sickles of pink. Rosy innards!
Papaya precious. At her feet, a child plays
in the sand with a knife, drawing scars
in the earth with ease.

The Call

"She came to me in a dream.
She said, *somebody from Canada
will touch your elbow, and you will know
you have to go.* This is how most calls
come, like rain in the night. You wake
with a chill and a memory of water
seeping into your dreams, leaving you sick
and tired of your own thirst.

She found me in an apartment in California
and broke down my door with a golden axe.
This is called Truth, she said, and pressed its edge
to my cheek. Why didn't I scream?
Why did I let her shave my head with her blade?
That's not what you do. In twenty minutes I was alone,
covered in a fine dust of myself. Sheared.
In mourning for me. After that I recycled.
I dreamed of castles made of old glass. I left my girlfriend
and walked the streets, saying *hey, hey!* to everyone
I met, hoping I'd unlock a secret code of west coast
spiritual dialect. In the end, it unlocked me. One month later
I was at a party and a stranger came up and embraced me,
grabbed my arms tight. I knew I had to go. I held on,
I wanted to go and I wanted to stay a little longer, holding him.
I needed a drink. I needed to be held.
She told me to let go, and go."

He Used To Be George

Now he is Krishna, meaning
dark skinned warrior
or flute, depending on who
you ask, meaning either
a delicate string of
violet and steely tin,
an instrument I refused to learn
as a child, or a man as dark
as a cold ocean, with the terrible
juvenile energy of a stone
which, flung carelessly
into a pond, spins farther
than you ever thought possible,
and the stone's earthly nature
becomes suspect, and you pinch
the warm slopes of your arm
searching for the source
of hidden mercury, or a slice
of a foreign planet, some injection
given to you at birth and designed
to mold you into this god, this boy
terrible, teenage hand of heaven,
hurling the earth away from his feet.

Catalogue

If I could list all the animals, I'd start with us.
We have the teeth, the claws.

The in-between times are best for creatures. I'm stuck
holding the sun up and the moon, dragging

me down, that old lady. That cold ball and silver chain.
I promised to hold her like a penguin and its moon full egg,

cupped on the curve of my foot. I hobble
pregnant with satellites, wonder

is my wandering equal to any path
the stars might take? I am a different kind

of slow burning body. I have a habitat,
somewhere in the forest. Someone's taking notes

on my behavior. Someone has plotted my migration
pattern, minds my breakfast cereal. I could see us

on TV someday, the greatest animals
ever discovered. I could see us mean. Wild.

Every Clean Beast

This morning I plucked tamarind
fresh from a low branch.
Swollen, resentful fruit, sour
as the eyes of the cow knelt
on the roadside, a beehive
waxing in her stomach. Somewhere
they've trained dogs to walk
into brain scanners. I live in fear
of the dead watching me.
Life is a lens, turning me gigantic
as a fresh mountain, still pink
from the womb. Thus magnified,
there is nothing to hide.

Drongo Ode

Dipping through the greenish scrub,
your quill tail tar black
and shadow dripping.
Bird of fluids.

At home in oil spills
and the hot breath of city air.
Your beak is the slit
of a church spire. Silent sewer.

While reading, I spied you
cutting afternoon light into wet cubes
that melt like gold butter onto my text.
You became my text, a little black
Q with a flourishing tail, coeval
creature to cursive and the burst
of dark grapes. In my sleep I will see you
slipping from shadow into subconscious,
your body a perfect V, for victory, vehemence,
a violent river, splitting with no warning.

Confession

It's natural to admire the body of a god
when his eyes are closed. I am a holy voyeur.
The presence of saints makes me forget
my pronouns. Frozen and guilty, I whittle myself
down to my petticoat, and his wife
is dragged away by demons.

Banana Leaf Scripture

We remember droughts
differently. The last time you had thirst,

my sand garden flourished. Populated
by jeweled people and shy crabs, we had

a really good year, people, profits are high
and we collected so many enemy heads.

Keep it up. This cyclical life of waves crashing
and money counting suited me and the birds

who heckled the stragglers and spat forecasts
from their birdteeth. This might have been a drought

but I remember only the beautiful jeweled people
and miles of sand, and prophecies raining from the sky.

It was always the same prophecy, the one that went
"It's all happening all over again!" That was comforting.

Some things you only believe when they're spat at you
from the sky. It's a system. It works and we flourished

and I don't remember any drought. I don't remember
anything but the flourishing, the jeweled people blinking

their perfect eyes, waiting for more omens, I don't remember
wanting anything but the next day to come,

I didn't know what thirst was
until you showed up, and started asking for water.

Body

of water, of weight,
I can't help singing to it,
    lovely
        miles of salt, crushed
    under the heel of a prehistoric, prescient
giant, who saw the bigger picture
every time she stood up to survey
the curvature of all surrounding
territories, and knew:
this can't be all there is,
 every horizon line
    disappoints at the same time
        excites at the same time
    as the land rushes up,
your body
is waiting
for a boat
an empty vessel
can only be filled
    through memory, likewise,
        when I say *attic*
    you think of your home,
the smell of lemon oil on oak
and the rustle of leaves falling
overhead, when I say *door*
you leave me and enter
your past.

We Were There At The Start And Saw How It Would Go

New life derived
from the dirt underfoot.
Ash. What is the word
for calm destruction?
We see the aftermath of time in the space
hollowed out in the forest's belly,
the tunnels of grief, a starved bear charging
out from within. One hop and skip
and you're in heaven,
or a hospital bed.
People, you pick your own doctors.
Mine left me voicemails, and I strained
to catch the instructions whispered
in the static at the end. It's always
at the end. Insects alight on skin,
gentle nudgings from the air. Little pushes.
That's all that's needed to seek help.

Making Breakfast After a Home Invasion

I.

There was a light on when I came home
and I thought nothing of it.

Cutting slices of fresh bread, I wiped each
with coconut oil and set them sizzling,

then took off my dress and listened to weird jazz.
A night of summer heat and peace, of broken fan blades

and dogs barking in the night. Yellow dogs standing
on the stone fence outside my window, howling

at nothing. The next morning was full of these echoes, the jeweled caviar
of a pomegranate's core. I have learned to shake its fruit loose

with the flesh facing away from my body
so that the juice stains the air, not my skin.

These smaller lessons orbit
the smaller life I live: *how to peel a papaya*
so the black seeds do not stick in your teeth. How to lead ants
across your floor, and out the door. How to sleep at night
when the dogs howl under the palm trees. How to listen,
how to understand the dogs at night.

II.

A subtle difference in their howls makes all
the difference. It is the same detail of the angle of the fruit turned

away from my body, the flesh swept clean. It is the shadow
passing across my window at night, and its import.

This morning, such a horror movie scene. Me, the red fruit clutched
in one hand, the blunt knife in the other,
bloody juice dripping through my fingers

as I realize a stranger had come and gone. *The killer, still inside!*
Drip, drip. What would I have done
if I happened to open the door and confronted- who? Done what?
What would have awaited me, in the light of the little room?
Instead of projecting futures, I examine the past, scouring f
or the signs I should have heeded. They appear quickly,

bobbing like buoys rising to the surface
signaling guilt and coming storms.

If I follow the trail back I might find all that I could have foreseen
and come the same conclusion, which means: how can I not

find myself like this, here in the future: *making fruit salad
on a warm morning in my house. Things that went missing.
Unlocked doors. Broken windows.
A dog barking in the night.*

Resource

You are salt. You make up
lesser mountains. Donkeys crawl
up your back, whining,
stumble down your spine.
Laden with you.
A scientist cut you from the earth
with an axe and it was
the best you've ever felt,
you cried so. She tasted you,
parceled you up in brown paper
packages and horse hair string,
sold you at every market
in the world. She sold you for
pennies. She sold you for an old car.
She sold you for her dinners,
she flavored her food with your body
and gave thanks to no one,
not even you.

High Definition

It's hard to imagine

being anyone else. I am not the woman
laying brown palms on the sand. I am not

the yellow putty of the church, holding a cross
behind my collarbone. I am not the numbered grid

of the map's edge, I do not have pretty creases
up my sides. I cannot be folded easily.

I am not the spider hiding in the bananas.
I am not the incense swimming through the room,

draping sweaty arms around white shoulders.
My scent does not induce sleep. I do not smolder,

I do not give you dreams. I am not the angel hair
of fishing nets drying in the sun. I am not the canal,

seeping down the city's spine, I am not the city,
nameless, alone, shivering in two.

Girl I

She is this drink I stir. The sweep
of cut straws over my surface, cleaning
me abrasively. I want to say, *I value you.*

With you it's like being alone. The best
possible compliment. They don't come easy,
these friends. These girls talk like it's

the fourth of July, and we love our country.
Nation building is a sport to her. We pieced together
our own island ages ago. I swim around it in circles.

She inhabits it, and calls me to shore with conch shells
and smoke signals. I see that cloud of black air in my
beach blue sky, that ball of red wool in my pocket,

a reverse unraveling. It's this love, a word
without the prickles of sex. This want is body-less.
I over-use that word with her. I throw it on the ground

and run over it, I want to pave the streets with it
and stomp until it's pressed into our landscape,
until it's breathless and casual as cement.

Girl II

She is that drink I stir. That field
we pass on the way home every night. It is a clearing
rimmed with white birches, stark lines of tree bodies
like steam escaping from cracks in the soft earth.

She once said she saw a phoenix rise from that clearing,
and even though she was making it up we could see it too.
Think of little girls picturing a phoenix. Who told us about these birds
on fire? I didn't picture it on fire, but glad. Whoever gets to burn
like that must be glad, rising like clockwork. That field.

I think it would be cool. I think it would be soft as blue velvet,
impervious to wrinkles and time. The fabric of that field stretches
in my mind, offers its body, a blanket to press my cheek to.
It's a place I've never been, but I want to return to, again and again,
until I have a reason to stop, and let myself in.

Girl III

She is this drink I stir.
We are royal in our exclusion
of everything else. Most kingdoms are made
from exiles, and we fling them off left and right.
We ignore each other's history.
We remember important dates.
We strive to look at the same clock. It circles
both of our wrists, her right, my left. I feel the ticking
like a copper pulse, grounding us in the same
time zone. We are shackled by our hair.
We apply coconut oil and watch it slide
and slip between our strands. We use the same
substances. Our skin tastes bitter at first, and then sweet
as cocoa butter, mellow and wet. We watch each other change.
We are aware of the shapes we make, we are a still life
of lime and papaya. We are a still life of egg
and dough, caked with flour. We are a still life
of an empty table. We are a form of expression.
We use the same products, we interchange our nails
and dust our eyelashes. We consider all social commentary.
We read current events as they unfold, inform each other of updates
on private and public lives. We read the same books,
we scorn the same magazines. We talk late at night
about justice and peace and we feel we are the beginning
of a new era under the sheets. We clue people in
to the dialogue of our candlelight. We take turns driving.
We are finely tuned to the radio. We have a frequency.
We have a vacation home on the airwaves. We are each other's filter,
ensuring we breathe cleanly. We dance. We stretch,
we shake our sheets free of dust.
We examine our skin. We take long drives
and discover new coasts. We feed stray dogs our scraps,
we wince at the shadows of crows. We watch the evening news
at six and when we turn the television off, we can feel
a buzz under our skin. We are sleuths. We know all the hiding places
and never lose each other. We wait. We rise. We sleep and wake up
in new places, we rule with a kindness
I never knew we had.

The Way Back

I have a line drawn in red across my chest
to remind me: don't hold things too close.
This morning of Indian rain, or the fire

at the foot of the mountain, where we stared
at each other's faces over the flame until
our features blurred and became candlelight,

and the sight of you stung. To wake in a foreign land
is to sleep in the past, in memories of familiar
places of rest. I sleepwalk backwards, board a plane.

I am the quiet passenger, curled up in the back of a taxi,
the slippery leather pressing lines in my cheek. I sprawl,
an unaware vagrant riding a dream

across the railways of the foothills
just to topple from the tracks
and curl into myself at the foot of a tree

to let the falling maple leaves cover me wetly—
a thin, sweet blanket. To wake, drenched,
ask the earth where I've been.

Carolyn Supinka is a writer, artist, and arts manager. Her work seeks to insert poetry and art into the everyday. Using visual art and public poetry projects, she investigates the shifting relationships between people, space, religion, and identity. From August 2013 to May 2014 she was a Fulbright-Nehru Scholar in Pondicherry, India, where she used poetry and art to investigate modern day spiritual journeys and cultural exchange. *Stray Gods* was written during her time in Pondicherry. Her poetry has been published at *Poet Lore, The Maynard, The Allegheny Review,* and *Fjords Review*, and she is a co-founder of the *VIATOR* project, a public literary and art journal. She was nominated for a Pushcart Prize in 2013 and in 2015.

http://cargocollective.com/carolynsupinka

www.ingramcontent.com/pod-product-compliance
Lightning Source LLC
Chambersburg PA
CBHW060226050426
42446CB00013B/3192